AF480629

EXPLORING THE LIFE AND IMPACT OF ANGELINA JOLIE

EXPLORING THE LIFE AND IMPACT OF ANGELINA JOLIE

ELARA PHOENIX

CONTENTS

CHAPTER 1

Disclaimer

The content in this book is intended for informational and entertainment purposes only. While every effort has been made to ensure the accuracy of the information presented, the author and publisher make no representations or warranties of any kind, express or implied, about the completeness, accuracy, reliability, suitability, or availability with respect to the content of this book.

The views and opinions expressed in this book are those of the author and do not necessarily reflect the official policy or position of any individual, company, or organization mentioned. Any resemblance to actual persons, living or dead, or actual events is purely coincidental.

This book is not intended to defame, libel, or slander any person, company, or organization. All references to individuals, companies, products, and brands are for illustrative purposes only, and no affiliation with or endorsement by them is intended or implied.

The author and publisher disclaim any responsibility for any actions or outcomes resulting from the application of information contained in this book. Readers should seek professional advice or conduct their own research when making decisions based on the content provided.

CHAPTER 2

Introduction

When one encounters Angelina Jolie's biographies today, she is celebrated as the Helen of Troy of the tabloids, the necrologue. She had it all - apparent perfection (or apparent disaster) in love affairs, in natural beauty and, when she had cancer, apparent disaster in health, too. Her life treasures (i.e. her six kids) commingle with her life tribulations (i.e. her six kids), as if in a B-movie about Christine Jorgensen. This is not surprising as what we find in biographies or memoirs, whether of biographers or self-writ, is just the person we are talking about - put in a good light. In Lesleyan: Angelina Jolie, we include the portrait of Jolie-as-Hollywood Star. I call her the 'kissstick,' fulfilled, high-fashion Cinderella in an exclusive, hops of every newscycle - 'AWW!' At her sumptuous estate with her litter of pixie-cut-mothered young bloods, on bended knee beside her loveblings, snogging the tweedy, sald-toughy Roland... Jolie-as-Hollywood Star has her malevolent charms, for even as I say this I am sorely tempted to follow it with a barrage of the sort of facts that defend a people's skeptical 'Gimme a break!'

Angelina Jolie has a dual persona. One she aspired to as a little girl when she first encountered the art of cinema and long before she was known, not as the woman who won every prize there is, but as one who changed the world. She was famous for being famous, one half of a smoochy, glamorous A-list couple who became Hollywood's 'humanitarian superstar', famous now because she was good. This essay revisits, in the spirit of the cover stories of Hello and OK! tabloids, the life, legacy, and impact of Angelina Jolie.

Background and Early Life

Angelina Jolie was born Angelina Jolie Voight on June 4, 1975, in Los Angeles, California, to an Academy Award-winning actor, Jon Voight. She made her screen debut as an uncredited infant in the film Lookin' to Get Out (1982), which her father starred in. She appeared with her father in the seafaring action film featuring pirates, across the 'war-stressed' Indian Ocean of 2003, Beyond Borders (2003), in which Angelina began to exert influence internationally, successfully and shortly before the film's release.

Angelina Jolie is one of the world's best-known individuals today. She has made over 50 films as an actress and has a net worth of $125 million as of 2022. Others view the celebrity as a role model who boasts a variety of appealing characteristics. It is frequently theorized about her personal experiences, contributions, and job offerings. Angelina Jolie is not just an actor; she even though throughout her personal life and humanitarian work. She has made significant contributions to those in need and has met more than 40 countries worldwide. Angelina Jolie is the subject of this report. Tshimo Moso Students were only thrived to be able to study their work. This piece discusses Jolie's background, early years, and formative experiences that contributed to their growth.

Rise to Stardom

Although her early acting career was defined as much by her off-screen, tabloid persona as by her on-screen performances, Angelina Jolie is today a prolific director and co-founder of the Maddox

Jolie-Pitt Foundation, which was established to "help rural Cambodians strive towards their quality of life, based on sustainable and ecologically sound development in their townships/villages." Her mother's untimely loss to ovarian cancer also inspired Jolie to create the Women in the World Foundation with New York Times journalist, Nicholas Kristof in 2012. The organization supports global women's rights by working to amplify the voices of oppressed and endangered women through its annual Women in the World summit.

Jolie found herself ready to step out of her father's shadow in 1998, when she starred in the television adaptation Gia telling the story of Gia Marie Carangi, a lesbian drug addict, sex addict, and supermodel stating, "The reason I did Gia wasn't just the nude scenes. It was everything about her. After we finished the movie, I couldn't stop setting cups on the table the way she did. I couldn't stop smoking the way she did." She swept up the awards for Best Actress that year, including Golden Globe, Blockbuster Entertainment, and SAG trophies. Her performance in this film was a seismic revelation. Gia presented to audiences, for the first time, the full complement of the Actor Studio skills she'd spent the past 18 months wielding in service of the Arnett script: the nudity, the androgyny, the emotional vulnerability, the raw sexuality, and the brooding silence. Gia entered Jolie's bloodstream much as it did Carangi's would-be lovers and admirers. The character's trauma and the inevitable, tragic denouement in substance abuse precipitated mach speeds of emotion for Jolie that resembled nothing so much as the profound emptiness that had often characterized her personal life. A decade earlier, she had pursued her solo career separate from her father's, launching an autumn campaign for Guess Jeans, where we find her lying naked amongst a field of wheat, her pubescent breasts, albeit mostly obscured, looking obliterated by time. In the rear of this semi-erotic, flat image shot on a black-and-white camera, the text reads, "Gia, Before She Was Famous?/Guess?: July 18th, 1978." In both the photo and the television movie Pollock, one of her later collaborations with Billy Bob Thornton, also encased on a flier, she is wheeling around Annette.

CHAPTER 3

Humanitarian Work

Shortly after she took on her role as Lara Croft, she joined the United Nations High Commissioner for Refugees (UNHCR) on a field mission. Realizing she could use her platform to bring serious global attention to the plight of people living in crisis areas, in 2001 Jolie became a United Nations (UN) Goodwill Ambassador for Refugees. Angelina Jolie is known the world over as an A-list movie star with countless accolades and awards to her name. But in addition to her undoubtedly impressive career in Hollywood, Jolie has also worked tirelessly for almost two decades for a number of global causes, leading many of her fans to admire her as much for her charitable endeavors as for her performances. The eldest daughter of Academy Award-winning actor Jon Voight and actress Marcheline Bertrand, Jolie was born on June 4, 1975. She began acting at a young age and has appeared in films such as Girl, Interrupted (1999), Lara Croft: Tomb Raider (2001) and its 2003 sequel, A Mighty Heart (2007), the Maleficent franchise, and more. In addition to her acting career, Jolie is an accomplished director, screenwriter, and film producer. She was named the highest-paid Hollywood actress in 2009, 2011, and 2013 according to Forbes.

Her mother cultivated this interest in philanthropy, taking Jolie to witness operations in areas with landmines and other hazardous remnants of war. Her experience soon surpassed her mother's, however, and Jolie was soon pursuing international work on her own. In the meantime, she let her career continue to evolve, with a mix of commercial blockbusters appended by visually ambitious passion projects like the historical biopic A Mighty Heart. Overall, Jolie and Pitt's long friendship with the philanthropist network has been lucrative, with PAJ Inc. utilizing the connections in their promotional materials to solicit donations for it. According to the MOU, proceeds are supposed to go to hospitals in developing countries imagined in the promotional materials, but beyond that oversight is flimsy at best.

UNHCR Goodwill Ambassador

"Angelina Jolie is one of the most widely recognized people around the world, as well as one of the most powerful people in the entertainment industry." Now in her mid-40s, she has spent the last decade involved in humanitarian work, serving as a UNHCR Goodwill Ambassador and, since 2012, a Special Envoy. Her famous face and powerful voice have raised the profile of the UN refugee agency to an unprecedented level. According to a media spokesperson, one implication is that "UNHCR commands more respect now. Humanitarian issues in general, and refugees in particular, can rarely get the same column inches in the world's media that accompanied Jolie and Pitt as they traveled the world visiting refugee camps and talking to UNHCR staff." This signifies a shift in how the general public and many diplomats perceive the work of the UN Refugee Agency as a result of Jolie's active involvement in the organization. That Angelina Jolie has been able to transform herself from a 'Hollywood bad girl' with a penchant for tattoos and attention-grabbing antics to a figurehead for humanitarianism is of wide-ranging relevance.

The Goodwill Ambassador position originally was established to capitalize on the fame and funds of celebrities for diplomatic ends. In movies crossing several continents, she portrayed a humanizing and compassionate image of the UN refugee agency, and she told The Washington Post, "I feel a sense of responsibility as the actor, when I leave films particularly, to keep the stories going about the part of the world I portray in a movie." UNHCR placed the 'right amount of distance' between her and the organization to safeguard it against allegations of using celebrities and to underscore the seriousness of the cause.

Founding the Jolie-Pitt Foundation

In order to further their activism, in 2006, Jolie and Brad Pitt founded the Jolie-Pitt Foundation, contributing millions of dollars to a wide range of activities. The foundation has supported the education, health, advocacy, and community development efforts of many organizations across the globe. The foundation is named after Jolie's children and is aimed at eradicating extreme rural poverty. Holistic approach. Jolie and Pitt acknowledged that although they could bring in a lot more resources than usual, such an effort might remain a drop in the bucket if they sat alone. At the Robin Hood Finale in New York City, An Evening Remembering Our Fallen Soldiers, Jolie said, "If we could work, in some small way, alongside other organizations that were planting individual trees, we could collectively reforest the entire ground."

In 2008, Jolie was given the Land O'Lakes Global Citizenship Award, which was established to honor the indomitable spirit of Wendell Willkie, who encouraged the transformation of the agriculture sector into a force that co-created better industries from a wellness trustworthy, knowledgeable base of men whose practices, attitudes, and economic partnerships contributed to the betterment of the global community. Exemplifying the power of many, Jolie and Pitt together received an award for their collaborative work as philanthropists during The Marcus Awards. Stojilska referred to Jolie as an "Oscar-winning philanthropist," an introduction to the speech. Jolie-Pitt Foundation's Beyond Shelter program works with local partners to provide a place of clear water, shelter, sanitation, health, and social services to families returning to their destroyed and often unlivable villages in the AdDa'a zone in Ethiopia. In the Agam area, in the autonomous Region of Eritrea, among returning refugees, hostility war displaced, and people who have been made internally homeless in former villages now entirely abandoned, it provides an important health outreach and volunteer point.

CHAPTER 4

Film Career

Education and First Marriages

Jolie pursued studies at the Lee Strasberg Theater Institute, where she later appeared in a number of stage productions and music videos by the mid-1980s. She took a break from show business following her first marriage to actor Jon Lee Miller in 1996. Jolie decided to recommit to acting after divorcing Miller in 2000. In 1999, she married actor Billy Bob Thornton, but their surprising divorce in 2003 was finalized in 2005.

Film Career

Actor Jolie first garnered attention for her performance in the 1998 film Gia, based on the short tragic life of model Gia Marie Carangi, who died from AIDS. The Los Angeles-based actress has also dabbled in modeling. In 2000, she appeared in the music video for rapper Korn's "Did My Time." In 1999, Jolie won an Academy Award for Best Supporting Actress for her role in Girl, Interrupted. The film was based on the true story of Susanna Kaysen, who spends 18 months in a psychiatric hospital. Jolie portrayed a sociopathic character named Lisa, who becomes her friend. She made her first appearance in an action film with the movie Lara Croft: Tomb Raider in 2001. Jolie played the title character, who fought men and monsters alike as a modern-day female Indiana Jones.

Jolie starred in Beyond Borders in 2003 as a girl who embarks on a cross-continental trip to help people in war-torn areas. The film was based on the true-life story of aid worker Wladyslaw Pasikowski. Jolie played a pilot and mother held hostage by a mercenary-pirate in 2010's The Tourist. The film also starred actor Johnny Depp. In 2014, Jolie was featured in "Maleficent," the revamp of the Sleeping Beauty fairytale from the villain's perspective. In 2015, Jolie starred in By the Sea with husband Brad Pitt. Based on Jolie's screenplay and directed by her, she and Pitt played on-screen husband and wife.

Breakthrough Roles

Her turn in the 1999 film Girl, Interrupted has remained one of Jolie's most memorable and iconic performances. Her portrayal of sociopath Lisa Rowe in this film earned her the Academy Award for Best Supporting Actress, making it her "breakthrough" role. This was the first time that a member of the Jolie family had won an Academy Award. It was also an important time in Angelina Jolie's career as an actress. Her role in this film proved that she was more than just Jon Voight's daughter.

Though the role of Lara Croft in 2001's Lara Croft: Tomb Raider originally garnered a mixed critical reception, the film as a whole was a commercial success and is widely considered to be Jolie's "breakthrough" part. Jolie earned her first BAFTA Awards nomination for Best Actress in a Leading Role for her performance in the film. Tomb Raider made it clear to producers that Angelina Jolie was a capable leading lady in a big budget action film and also helped to market her public image. So even though it was not a huge commercial hit, it boosted her value in Hollywood. Director Simon West initially turned down Jolie for the part, but he changed his mind when she sent him a blood-soaked letter with the tagline: "I will come to your house and kill you if I don't get this role." Daniel Craig, her costar in the film, publicly stated in 2011 that he and Jolie never got on while making the film. "I was overwhelmed by her and was not overly happy with the film," stated Craig.

Acclaimed Performances

Despite the mixed reviews of Changeling, Jolie's work in the film received immense acclaim. Critics were entranced by her performance and her ability to transform and depict a variety of human emotions. Todd McCarthy writes that "Jolie delivers a powerful performance that is definitely things-behind-the-eyes as well as physical, fearfully and poignantly portraying a woman assailed on all sides by male power and inhumanity." Cathy Dunkley praised her ability and likened her to renowned Hollywood actresses. "As a mother up against a male-dominated 1920s LAPD, Angelina Jolie rated an encouraging number of mentions for her fiercely emotional performance," she commented. "Oscar's a long shot, but Clint Eastwood's heart-wrenching period drama looks to be well placed in a season already crowded with potential contenders," wrote Peter Travers of Rolling Stone. "Angelina Jolie brings all the elements of her movie-star allure to the title role," commented Richard Corliss of Time. On a performance standpoint, she's shown us everything she has gained from great coaching and all her years in the emotional-straitjacket industry." Richard Schickel of Time also praised Jolie and compared her to an era of actresses, not in terms of ability, but in terms of the "informed stillness" Schickel suggests they possess. "Something else," writes Schickel. "Angelina Jolie alone among current American leading ladies (in this film, anyway) reminds us of the sort of acting we used to see on screen generations ago, the 'informed stillness' that could be discerned behind the Plaster of Paris masks, by the accomplished performers who wore curtain-call roles with introspective silence, by the stars who figured everything when you saw nothing."

Jolie's outstanding performance in A Mighty Heart was frequently praised and received numerous accolades and nominations. New York Times writer A. O. Scott praised Jolie and said, "She is as committed and honest in her way as her character is in hers, and that character, Ms. Pearl, forces her to face the limits of her talent in a way no role before has, and she responds overtly." Similarly, Variety's Joe Leydon said that Jolie "delivers a detailed performance as the anguished widow of murdered journalist Daniel Pearl." On June 21, 2017, Mary McNamara of The Los Angeles Times gave Jolie a positive review, saying, "Her take on Rand is that she is a woman who never hesitates, and Jolie is a great fit for this complicated character, a dominant geopolitical force who still won't think twice about raiding a private stash of French perfume." Ray Bennett of The Hollywood Reporter attended the movie premiere on May 17, 2017, and said Jolie's "dramatically flashy performance is out of a classic Bette Davis melodrama." J. Hoberman of The Village Voice described her acting as "pure Sarah Bernhardt" and added that her performance is "by far the most entertaining thing about Changeling is Jolie and her alternately histrionic and awe-struck admirers." Jurnee Smollett, one of Jolie's co-stars, said, "[Angelina] does amazing work" and praised her "fierce work, brave work," adding, "[This is] probably one of Angelina's most powerful performances." Changeling grossed $113m.

Personal Life

Jolie collects knives and has an affinity for tartan clothes. In the early 1990s, she suffered from depression and planned to commit suicide twice. She experienced a nervous breakdown after her mother's death, and began to self-harm as an act of self-healing. In an attempt to reconcile her love for her then-husband Billy Bob Thornton, Jolie was removed from the location of their 2001 film Bandits for "unreasonable behavior" on the set. Her attempts to join the fashion business caused a negative reaction in 2014.

Jolie allegedly had a brief relationship with actor Timothy Hutton in 1998, who became a temporary caregiver for her adopted son Maddox in the absence of Daniel and Martin. Her brother James Hewitt supports her during her difficulties, and there is also speculation that she has embarked on a new relationship with her. Jolie refers to actor and model Jenny Shimizu as a friend who was once part of a loving relationship with her. Jolie and Thornton married on May 5, 2000, and co-starred in the comedy film, Pushing Tin. Adopted daughter James and Elizabeth's baby Maddox accompany James and Elizabeth. In 2003, Jolie and Thornton announced their separation and divorce, and Jolie confirmed that she is pregnant with their child. According to FHM magazine, she is the sexiest woman in the world and has twice topped her list. In 2004, Jolie was known as the third most powerful actress in the world and the most powerful at the age of 21. In 2007, Forbes listed her as the fifth most influential person in the entertainment industry, the 14th highest-paid actress in the world, and the world's most influential woman. In 2012, she was the fourth most powerful artist in the world.

Family and Relationships

Angelina Jolie is a mother and an artist. Although she grew up watching her mother on set and living in the public eye, Jolie has managed to carve out a rather eclectic career as an actress and UN-HCR Ambassador, with her love for humanitarian work occupying most of her time. Away from the camera, Jolie is known for her large family, made up of children from around the globe who Jolie describes as 'of the same blood', specifically her ex-husband Brad Pitt's adopted children, Maddox Chivan, Zahara Marley, and Pax Thien, and their biological children Shiloh Nouvel, Knox Léon and Vivienne Marcheline. Jolie's mother, actress Marcheline Bertrand, passed away in 2007 after battling ovarian cancer. Despite being estranged from her father, actor Jon Voight, Jolie stated that she held no ill feelings towards her father and often found herself defending him. Despite not having contact with Voight for nearly a decade, after the death of her mother, Jolie and her father reconciled.

During the twenty seasons the show has been in production, The Prices are Right has gifted contestants with hundreds of cars, lavish trips, dream homes and even millions spent in giveaways. In 2009, a then-pregnant Shiloh Jolie-Pitt appeared on a jumbotron in a Malawian orphanage to announce her country's own humanitarian good will in the form of a new school, named the Shiloh Jolie-Pitt Academy. More often than not, though, Jolie's background and relationships are an afterthought in the shadow of her ex-husband, Brad Pitt. In June of 2005, less than a year after Pitt and Aniston divorced, Angelina Jolie told Marie Claire: 'It took until Anything.' During the shoot, the soon-to-be-couple took advantage of their alone time together to begin cohabitation, selling the home they shared in Los Feliz, California before officially adopting their first child, Maddox, then 5, less than a year later. Pitt and Jolie never married during the span of their decade together, despite sharing six children, but were in a committed relationship, referred to as a 'marriage' by the parties involved and standing as such in their relationship to the children, until filing for divorce- co-ownership of assets having established.

CHAPTER 6

Media Image

Jolie's image is gleaming as a saint who exudes goodness and sex appeal, and when she suddenly became tabloid tailoring herself as "the wife of Mr. Smith," Jolie's reputation as a relentless man harvester tabloid plaything was powerless to stop this amazing transformation. Media have the ability to form the public's perception of public figures, and it is of little surprise how much Jolie's career has taken off considering the overly attractive image culminated around her due to the excessive tabloid coverage. Through the production of a foundation for an unsinkable media image and the attraction of press, Jolie managed to reach an unsuspected level of fame.

Angelina Jolie had been able to command the tabloids to her benefit, changing her image from a troubled bad girl with a turbulent past and tendencies to wear vials of blood around her neck to a reformed mother of the world. A part well planned because she, unlike most modern celebrities, controls what the public knows about her. During the filming of Beyond Borders, the story of a couple in love who are torn apart by their dedication and passion to save starving children, Jolie's then-latest pet project, she underwent an extreme transformation; malicious Angelina became a UN humanitarian. Her character in the film contains more than just a little bit of the good that Jolie put into every humanitarian mission of hers, this is quite a statement for a film that is marketed as being based on true events. Angelina Jolie has an amazing impact, as both a movie star and a celebrity. Her well-dressed image as a mother of the world, with fierce intelligence, great love, and good intentions are irresistible to the media. When it comes to Jolie, every piece of information turns into good news for the developing countries of the world. It started with her Vietnamese adoption of son Maddox in 2002.

Public Perception

Angelina Jolie is one of those people who feels deeply connected to her sense of self and spent a considerable amount of time and energy developing her professional abilities. She is often described as brilliant. Perhaps she has been successful because loyalty to herself is paramount: she sticks to her principles and does not veer from them. Unfortunately, the media often outright lies about the personal and professional life of a public figure, and Jolie is no exception. If it were not for trusted journalists who took the time to write well-researched material, it is unlikely that the average fan of Jolie would ever learn the truth about her. Especially when it comes to the famous, constructing a good image is essential for maintaining their celebrity status and career of good work. With several sources verifying a tale, it is much more difficult for a person's detractors to make up stories about them.

Another reason that no one can be "normal" when you are as famous or wealthy as Angelina Jolie is that she doesn't pause her acting career anymore. She could have dropped out of the business for a few years and simply shot films in her house to keep the paparazzi out of her hair if she wanted to lead a "normal" life. Keeping one's gob shut in the event of a personal tragedy is not any more dangerous for a hidden waitress grieving the loss of a beloved dog than it is for a celebrity staring at the loss of their child's life on the front page of The National Enquirer. And yet, the server can decide to whom her distress is conveyed and govern her children's exposure, whereas the starlet (or the president) must deal with the hands dealt to her.

Tabloid Controversies

The couple drew criticism for their previous relationships while Brad was married to Jennifer Aniston. Aniston fans and the tabloids that serve them evoked the image of Brad and Angelina as the new Liz and Dick, appropriating Elizabeth Taylor's image as one-half of the notorious public affair with Richard Burton to construct a textual makeover of Aniston as the saintly, wronged woman. The press also makes frequent reference to Angelina's openly bisexual past in interviews, generating as many variations and innuendos as possible on headlines alluding to Angelina as the 'sexiest woman alive.' The pregnancy became a large tabloid story in the summer of 2006, with the supermarket tabloid US and People magazine at the center of intense media competition leading up to, and following, the announcement of Jolie's due date.

Celebrities are and seem the same, but different when examined with the long boring gaze of the tabloids, where we are presented with fresh stories thinly disguised in the form of the bodies of celebrity culture. Angelina Jolie as superstar and mother has inspired the latest rage in tabloid continuities, in as hot a commodity as tabloids themselves are capable of manufacturing in her much-publicized, relatively brief coupledoms, film career, and now, family. The tabloids do not so much bend the truth as insist on a fundamental oscillation between "glurge and gore," the morally valid and depraved in the commentary on the image.

CHAPTER 7

Legacy and Influence

In 2005, Angelina Jolie discussed her dedication to her philanthropic work in a statement to Forbes, saying "When I first became UNHCR Goodwill Ambassador, I saw how you could make a difference in other people's lives. I've been struck by the fact that you need so little to give so much." Over 20 years later, the actress's work in the humanitarian sector has made a lasting impact on the world of philanthropy, influence, and Hollywood. In 2013, Jolie was named one of the 25 biggest female philanthropists in America. The actress's early work as a Goodwill Ambassador led to her participation in other larger global efforts. She has appeared in Namibia to raise awareness about AIDS, gone to Iraq to fight for Jordanian refugees, and appeared before the UN Security Council to urge the world to take special notice of the protection of women and children. This use of the star system to further global efforts is seen by some as the rise of "philanthropy as a second career" and has made Jolie one of the most influential celebrities at the table of global management. This is not to say that there has not been a fair share of criticism along the way, with many wanting to accuse Jolie of having succumbed to "vain charity" or of being hypocritical. However, despite the controversies, the power of star philanthropy is said to be more popular than ever and is likely to play a key role in the future.

In addition to her role in advocacy, Jolie is also influencing the film industry to prioritize the genres that reflect her passions - dramas and charitable films. In 2007, Jolie, along with Brad Pitt and Keith Vanderberg, an entertainment industry writer, founded Plan B Entertainment, a film production company. Under the hat of Plan B, Jolie was able to create works of art that reflected her own social and emotional concerns, such as A Mighty Heart, The Changeling, and In the Land of Blood and Honey, in which she examined the civil war in Bosnia. She has said, of her work with Plan B, "We want our films to have low box office expectations so they'll pay attention, and we also want them to be little surprises. That's why it works for us. We throw something out there and people get nervous and we make some beautiful films. And then we have a bigger audience for those films." Several of the films released by Plan B have received critical acclaim, but she also used the production company as a tool to help her philanthropic efforts.

Impact on Humanitarian Causes

Turning direct involvement in the fight into an international cause célèbre, Angelina Jolie helped to draw unprecedented attention to some of the most desperate areas of the globe. "People started calling me up and asking, 'What is she doing in Washington? Or Iraq? What's the impact of what she actually did?'" Kopp's Michael, then new partner, states. "In their characterization, we had caught lightning in a bottle."

Angelina Jolie was not unknown when her now famous Washington, D.C. dinner took place. A decade of film performances cemented her celebrity, turning her name recognition into an asset in recognizing other global hot spots. In the years since her Oscar win, she has used the platform it reinforced to build a broader portfolio of U.N. Goodwill Ambassador work. "In little more than a year,

Angelina Jolie has given more money and attention to stir up passion on behalf of the dispossessed than almost any other celebrity." In the past, celebrities had come and gone. Today, says Marc Biad in his capacities working with and for U.N. refugee experts, the organization almost can't do without them. Research into Angelina Jolie's role as Refugees chief from 2000-2009 and felt Jolie's steady glow at her side until 2012. Beyond awarding the woman who had done so much sculpting of the volume, many stories she left behind will have measurable legacies long into the future. Angelina Jolie has given voice to human rights and humanitarian issues.

Representation in Hollywood

Jolie certainly made a lasting impact in Hollywood, but few gushed about her legacy as a female director when she first started directing films. For the most part, Jolie made headlines as the "adulteress" who "broke up" Pitt's relationship with Jennifer Aniston. And her pregnancy with Shiloh was indeed hugely controversial, but mostly because it had the media speculating for months on whether she was pregnant or malnourished. While Jolie's radical lifestyle may have mismatched the typical mom next door image Hollywood loves to show even its A-list stars as, Jolie wasn't going to be pinned to that image.

Instead, she is the human we celebrate. Moreso than any of her films, her domestic harmony, her family planning, or the evolution of her image, though, Jolie is part of a very small handful of women helping to shape the representation and diversity, or lack of it, in Hollywood today. This is arguably her biggest legacy. Jolie has, for two decades, used her fame to elevate questions about the role and influence celebrities play in people's understanding of world events; she humanizes and champions the poor and those in war-torn countries forgotten by a world that couldn't comprehend the violence of their own making. She has worked to dismantle ideas of the political Hollywood star as someone muted by handlers and restricted to talking only on-set, and perhaps most of all, Jolie has been a woman who, alongside Malala Yousafzai and the late Samantha Smith and Shirley Temple, has shown us that women are both star-power and humanitarian ambassadors. In other words, Angelina Jolie has shown the world that bright women are also those that light their path towards greater justice and richer lives. She is Hollywood's Humanitarian Superstar.

CHAPTER 8

Conclusion

With acts of bravery, talent, and humanitarianism, Angelina Jolie changed from an unknown member of a famous Hollywood family to an international superstar. We embarked on a journey through her personal life, her preparation for a movie career, and her strides into the UN. Her career on the big screen is escalating, and her director's projects are stirringly received by impressed critics.

The things about Angelina Jolie are the impact she has made off the big screen. The actress tries to be a sort of stealth mom in her personal life, keeping her household in order, driving between schools and swimming pools for varying problems. She speaks readily, however, about the world's concerns, sets out to travel to dangerous places in order to realize what Hollywood celebrities go through. "Who wants to associate themselves with someone who bitches about hair and makeup all the time?" she said one time when explaining her reasons to make a conscious effort to step out of the limelight and back away from the mainstream Hollywood scene. Angelina's artistic endeavor, she says, is real life. "As good as we can make it be."

www.ingramcontent.com/pod-product-compliance
Lightning Source LLC
Chambersburg PA
CBHW050031110726
47973CB00024B/264